SIGNING
AT CHURCH
FOR ADULTS AND YOUNG ADULTS

BEGINNING SIGN LANGUAGE SERIES

D1279145

Designed and Illustrated by
Jane Schneider, Kathy Kifer, and Marina Krasnik

Special thanks to

BJ Hauck
for her help and guidance

Copyright ©1998 by Stanley H. Collins

Published by
Garlic Press
605 Powers Street
Eugene, OR 97402

www.garlicpress.com

ISBN 0-931993-98-9
Reorder Number GP-098

Introduction

Signing at Church should be used as a helpful signing tool in the church setting. It should help to bring hearing impaired and hearing church members closer in their exchange and in their worship.

Signing at Church presents a little of everything: phrases, common words, an index, a Bible passage, and the Lord's Prayer. Please note that phrases and passages vary in their exact signing translations: often understood words are omitted, but for significant passages, like the Lord's Prayer, nearly exact English is modeled.

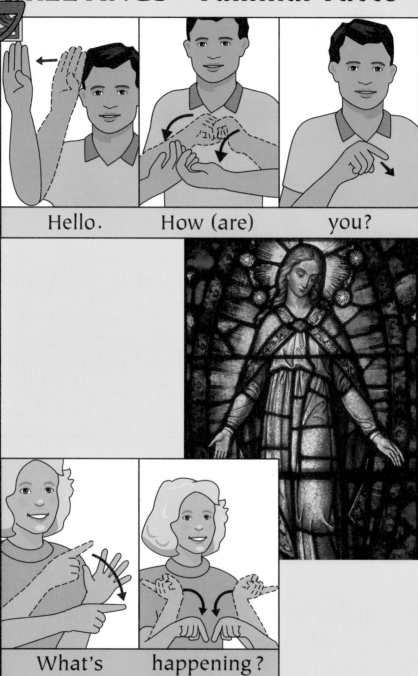

Hello. How (are) you?

What's happening?

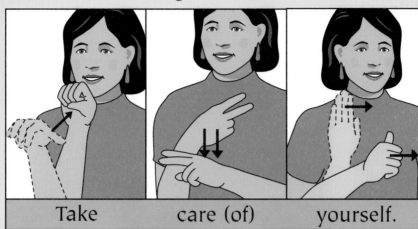

Take   care (of)   yourself.

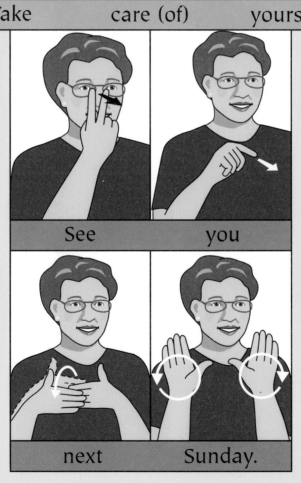

See   you

next   Sunday.

Haven't seen you

for awhile.

Welcome (to) our church.

My name (is) . . .

Use finger spelling when you don't know a sign. Names are good to finger spell.

Happy   (to) meet   you.

Have   you

come   here   before?

(Do) you   have   (any) questions?

(Do) you   want   (an) interpreter?

(Do) you   want   (to) go

(to) Sunday   School?

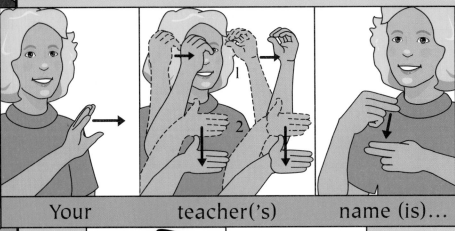

Your   teacher('s)   name (is)...

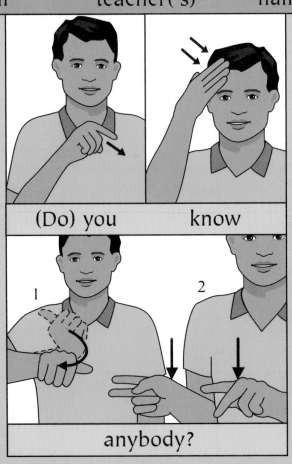

(Do) you   know

anybody?

How   old   (are) you?

What   grade   (are) you (in)?

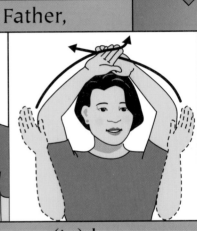

Our   Father,

who   art   (in) heaven,

hallowed   be

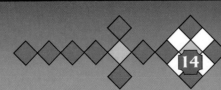

Thy name.

Thy Kingdom come.

Thy will (be) done

15

on   earth   as

(it is) in   heaven.   Give

us   this   day

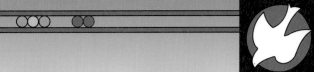

our daily bread.

And forgive us

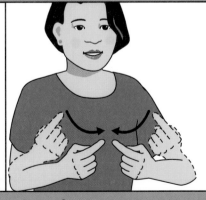

our trespasses

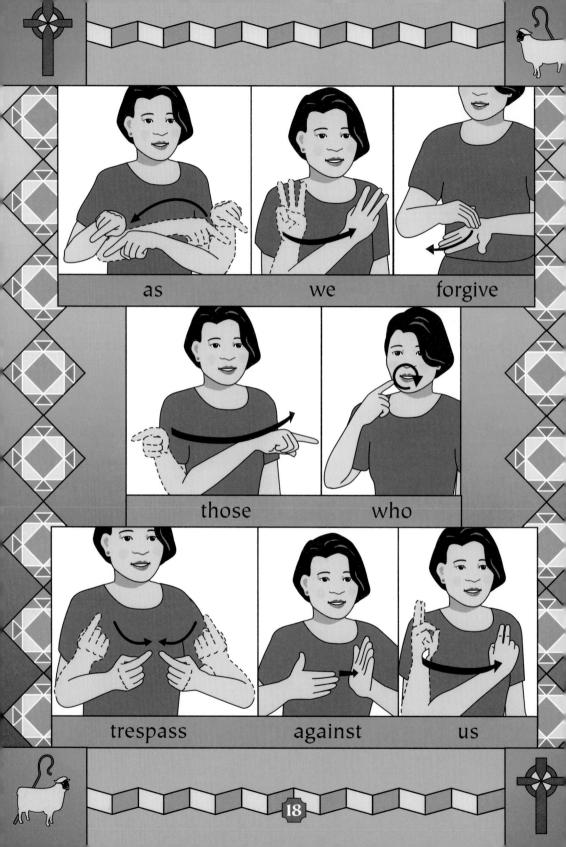

as   we   forgive

those   who

trespass   against   us

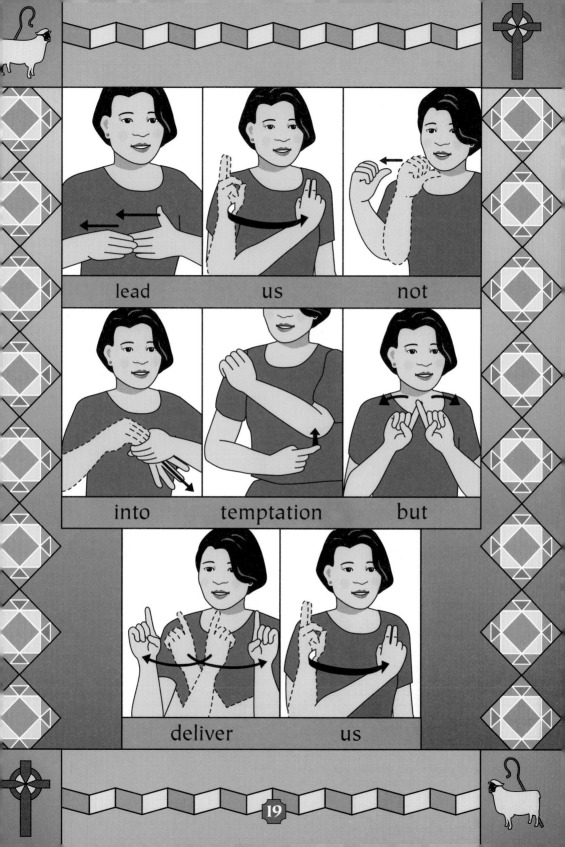

lead　　us　　not

into　　temptation　　but

deliver　　us

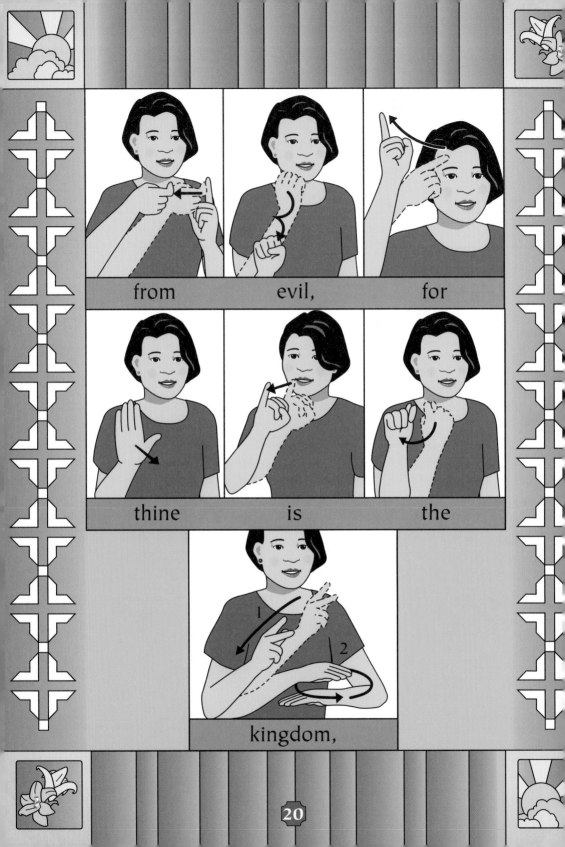

from   evil,   for

thine   is   the

kingdom,

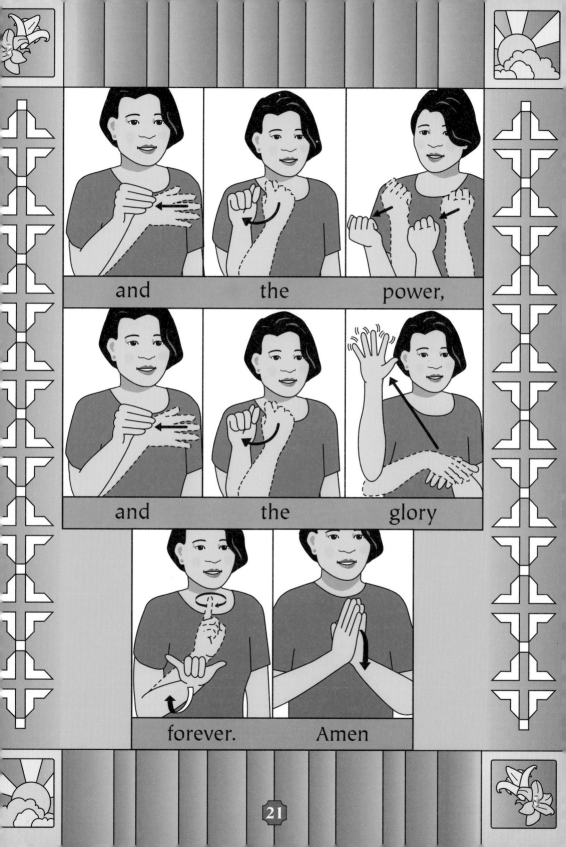

and　　　　　the　　　　power,

and　　　　　the　　　　glory

forever.　　　Amen

21

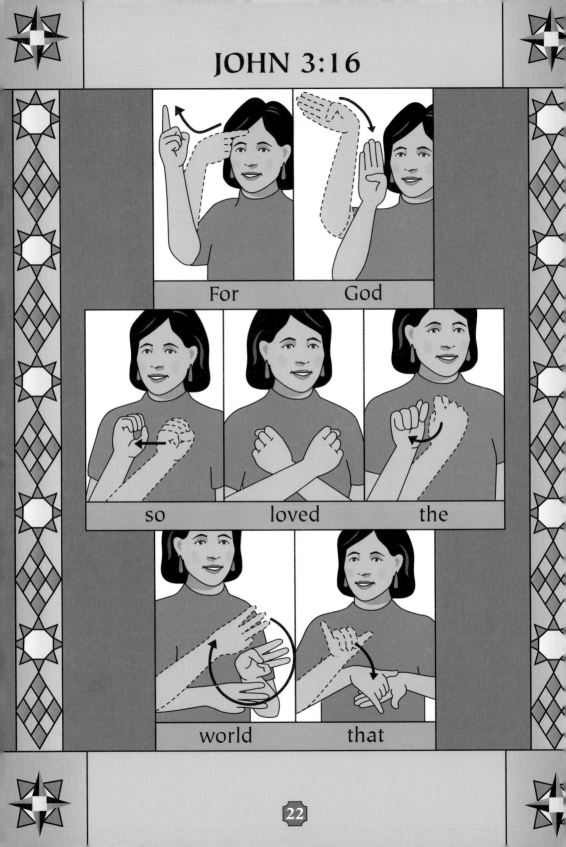

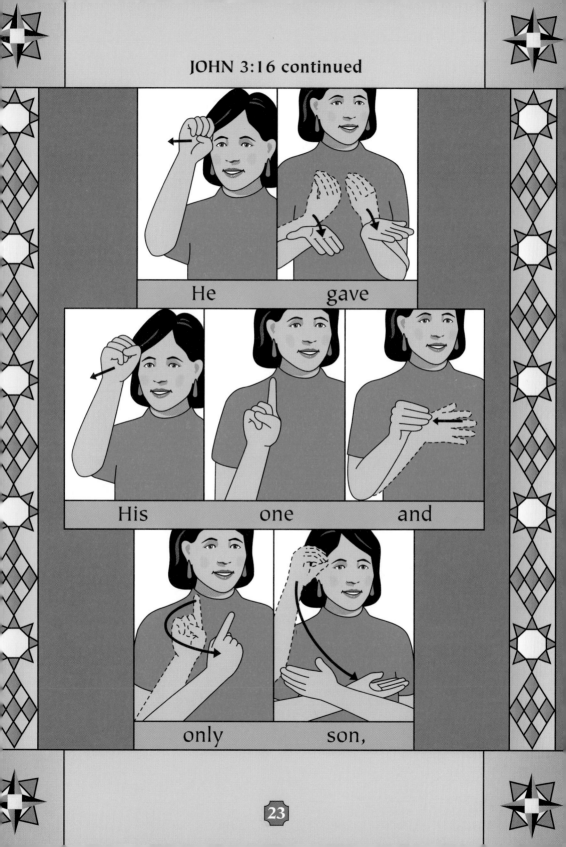

He   gave

His   one   and

only   son,

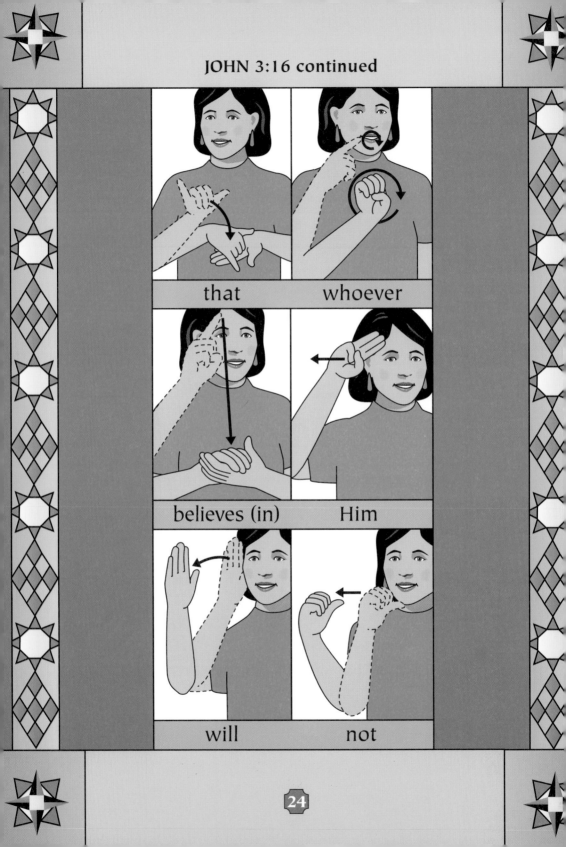

that whoever

believes (in) Him

will not

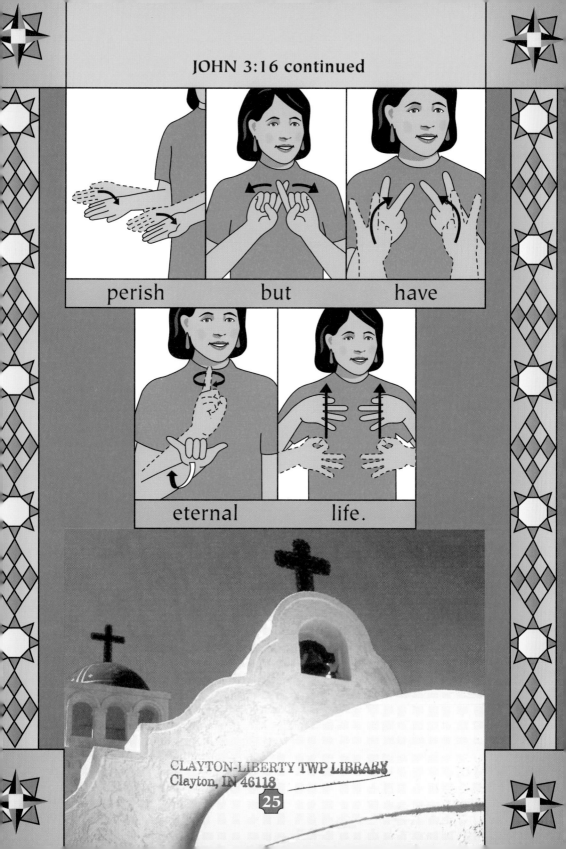

perish   but   have

eternal   life.

alleluia

amen

baptize

Bible

believe

bless

chapter

Christ

Christian

commandment communion cross

disciple Easter evil

faith | forgive | God

gospel | Holy Ghost/Holy Spirit

Jesus | joy | love

pastor, preacher

peace

pray

praise

priest

religion

resurrection

New Testament

Old Testament

worship

Index

Also from Garlic Press

Finger Alphabet GP-046
Uses word games and activities to teach the finger alphabet.

Signing in School GP-047
Presents signs needed in a school setting.

Can I Help? Helping the Hearing Impaired in Emergency Situations
GP-057 Signs, sentences and information to help communicate with the hearing impaired.

Caring for Young Children: Signing for Day Care Providers and Sitters
GP-058 Signs for feelings, directions, activities and foods, bedtime, discipline and comfort-giving.

An Alphabet of Animal Signs
GP-065 Animal illustrations and associated signs for each letter of the alphabet.

Mother Goose in Sign
GP-066 Fully illustrated nursery rhymes.

Number and Letter Games
GP-072 Presents a variety of games involving the finger alphabet and sign numbers.

Expanded Songs in Sign
GP-005 Eleven songs in Signed English. The easy-to-follow illustrations enable you to sign along.

Foods GP-087
A colorful collection of photos with signs for 43 common foods.

Fruits & Vegetables GP-088
Thirty-nine beautiful photos with signs.

Pets, Animals & Creatures
GP-089 Seventy-seven photos with signs of pets, animals & creatures familiar to signers of all ages.

Signing at Church
GP-098 For adults and young adults. Helpful phrases, the Lord's Prayer and *John 3:16*.

Signing at Sunday School
GP-099 Phrases, songs, Bible verses and the story of Jesus clearly illustrated.

Coyote & Bobcat
GP-081 A Navajo story serving to tell how Coyote and Bobcat got their shapes.

Raven & Water Monster
GP-082 This Haida story tells how Raven gained his beautiful black color and how he brought water to the earth.

Fountain of Youth
GP-086 This Korean folk tale about neighbors shows the rewards of kindness and the folly of greed.

Ananse the Spider: Why Spiders Stay on the Ceiling
GP-085 A West African folk tale about the boastful spider Ananse and why he now hides in dark corners.

www.garlicpress.com